Desree is an award-winning spoken word artist, writer and facilitator based in London and Slough. Artist in Residence for poetry collective EMPOWORD, and an Obsidian Foundation Alumni, Desree explores intersectionality, justice and social commentary. Desree is also the producer for both Word Up! and Word Of Mouth LDN, a TEDx speaker, and has featured at events around the UK and internationally, including Glastonbury Festival 2019, Royal Albert Hall and Bowery Poetry New York

I Find My Strength in Simple Things

Desree

Burning Eye

BurningEyeBooks
Never Knowingly
Mainstream

This second edition published by Burning Eye Books 2021

www.burningeye.co.uk

@burningeyebooks

Burning Eye Books
15 West Hill, Portishead, BS20 6LG

ISBN 978-1-913958-03-9

I Find My Strength in Simple Things

For George Carty and Maule Gumbs
Thank you. I hope I make you proud.

CONTENTS

NEVER FALL IN LOVE WITH A POET

They told me,
> *Never fall in love with a poet.*

They use their words like rope,
smother you with them till you choke,
but what a way to go.

I imagine we'd argue in metaphors.
Bring different meaning to
> *I'll show you mine*
> *if you show me yours,*
fall in love with every cause.

I'd wake up to Maya Angelou
notes on my pillow, Shakespeare
quotes on my window, and know
no other love has been this close.

I'd find Post-it notes that say,
> *Only the moon understands my pain*
> *because it too waits for its love,*
> *the sun, all day…*
> *Take the bins out,*
and I'll take the bins out.
Because I want to,
because I need you.

We'll never say *I love you,*
we both know this is more
than love, this is more than us,
we'll use words as hugs.

I won't fall in love with your face.
I'll fall in love with what you say.
I won't write poetry about
how your lips taste,
but how you penetrate
my brain.

We evolve
and revolve
around a universe
we made up.

It's just us.

BLACK GIRL MAGIC

It's easy to say know your worth
when your worth has been
so consistently defined.

When you aren't judged
by the texture of your hair,
the roll in your hips
or the way you cut your eyes.

When people can say,
She's angry,
and you're just angry;
it's not associated
with any stereotypes.

I am not an angry black woman.
I'm a Black Woman,
who sometimes gets angry.
Apparently, that's not okay.

Constantly being judged
by my tone, not what I say.

> *We are all entitled to our opinions,*
> *but don't say yours too loud.*
> *In fact, could you just tone it down?*
> *There are other people around.*

I have a telephone voice.
A sound I use to disguise
the Black that's on my skin.
If I make my tone a little bit softer,
make my pitch a little bit higher,
maybe it will disguise
some of the melanin
I'm drowning in.

I am loud.
I'm trying to be heard.
I do try to have the last word,
because you didn't listen to the first.

It's like we are not allowed
to be passionate or speak
with conviction. It's like
we are not allowed to be
strong or we're not entitled
to an opinion.

We don't even own our own beauty.

Big lips
aren't shit,
unless Kylie Jenner
has them.
A fat bum
isn't the one
unless it's
Kim Kardashian.

Black women
were in human zoos
until 1958.

That could have easily
been your mother,
standing behind that fence.
Being fed food by white dudes
who will never understand
the gravity behind these legs,
or the weight this ass has held.

You will see me get angry
if you ever tell me
I am pretty
for a Black Girl.

Why wouldn't I be angry?

History has taught us
nothing good has ever come
from this skin.
We are fantasised.
We are fetishised,
because everyone wants
to take a dip
in some melanin.

When will we get the respect we deserve?
We are good enough for your music videos,
but bad bitches need to be seen and not heard.

So, this is for
my Erykah Badus.
My Lauryn Hills.
My Maya Angelous.

My Floetry sisters.
My Harriet Tubmans.
My Shonda Rhimes.

My Black Women
who were
trod on like dirt.
But, like the dust,
they rise.

This for my Black Girls
who know they are not their hair,
or any other part of their anatomy.

This is for my Coretta Kings –
whose dreams might not be quotable
but left an imprint on our reality.

Sarah Reed.
Rest in peace.
A Black Woman,
in the UK,
'found' dead
whilst in custody.

But didn't have
enough testosterone
to incite a rally.

Black Girls, you are magic.
Black Girls, you rock.
Black Girls, stand.

It's time we start believing it
instead of just creating these hashtags.

Scan the QR code to watch
a video of this poem

DEFINING YOU

for Lucien

I have literally watched you grow.
When we were young,
we used to sit in front of the TV,
and I used to stroke the bottom
of your earlobes.

I don't know when you think
you became a man,
but there's a lot more
involved.
You've got a long way to go.
Don't let them rob you of your growth.

Your generation talks about
being the realest,
but ask the elders;
this is the fakest anyone
has ever seen the roads.

The hustle was birthed
from poverty.
Young entrepreneurs,
with no other options,
trying to gain a monopoly.

You've got a good head
on your shoulders,
and a really big heart.
Don't let the mistakes
you make define
who you are.

Young Black Boys,
listen: they don't want to
see you make it. They

see your dreams and
want to make sure
that's all they will ever be,

won't teach you how to
raise your hand in class,
but you know it's two hands
when you see the police.

In both situations,
you are seen as a threat.
But, once you find the key
to your potential, who knows
what's next?

That means trying.
Trying means doing
way more than surviving.

How are we supposed
to succeed in a world
that continues to profit
off the colour of our skin?

Self-hatred isn't new;
it was engrained in the enslaved,
as though it is part of our DNA,
built in.

I know what I'm asking you
doesn't sound feasible.
The TV told you cutting bricks
is the only way to make your
goals achievable.

Don't trust a system
that puts more Black Men in prison
than there ever were slaves.

Don't trust a system
that refuses to teach you
the difference between
wealth and being paid.

You cannot become a statistic.
We have worked too hard
and we have come too far.

Only you can define who you are.

Scan the QR code to watch
a video of this poem

JIGSAW

I made us a jigsaw puzzle.
Not only did it take time
to put together,
you are the only way
that I feel complete.
But every time you leave,
you take your piece.

When we're together,
you make it difficult to remember
that you have only loaned it to me.

Being number two
isn't hard
when number one
isn't around.

You make it easy to forget
that I'm playing second best,
that I'm reserved to the bench.
During training I get to play,
but I'm barely acknowledged
on match day.

I can't do this.

I can't just match the pieces,
hoping you give yours to me.
My heart is fighting
with my sanity.
I'm unable to think
about this rationally.

Your love hurts.
It's damaging me.

How can I love you
more than I love myself
when your love is not mine?

I wish that giving up
was easier than trying.

I wish I didn't want you.
I wish I could love myself
enough to realise
leaving would mean
a lot less pain,
a lot less shame,
a lot less finding someone else
to blame.

I do not want to let go.
I just want to own
the piece you've given
to me on loan.

I became home
for everything you
didn't share with her.
My soul became your storage,
so, even if I wanted to leave,
nothing in here belongs to me.

It is all yours.
This relationship is all doors;
you're the only one with the keys.

You come and go
as you please,
ensuring each time
you leave, you've left
enough room for
my insecurities.

I know it will never be me.
That's why I've never
asked you to choose.

I guess it's that shit they say about the grass.

No matter how many pieces I keep,
she'll always have the peace I need.

Maybe it's time to take this jigsaw apart.

Scan the QR code to watch
a video of this poem

DEAR MS WILLIAMS

I am not trying to start
a feminist movement.
I am not trying to incite
a race riot.
In a world that
should be ours
it's really hard
to remain quiet.

How dare they call her
anything less than Queen?
Anything less than the best
tennis player this world
has ever seen?

Success started to look
a little bit like me,
and I'm reminded,
no, she can't be pretty.

They appropriate our culture.
Tell us a big bum's nice,
but only if the skin's light.
This is more than
a few squats at the gym.
This is thousands of years
of lineage.
This is the arse
that built the pyramids.
And they call her masculine?

Can't they see that those legs
were made for those hips?
Those thighs were made to crush shit
like countless world championships.

Yet they belittle her success.

Telling little Black Girls everywhere,
their accomplishments will always
be worth less.

But, Ms Williams,
even when they try
to crush your spirit,
you're the type of woman
that I'd like to be.
They can try to take
everything from you,
but they'll never take away
your dignity.

And that arse.
And those hips.
And them thighs.
And those splits.
And your swing.
And your serve.
And your pride.
And your worth.

Fuck being a model
when you can be an icon.
Whether you got Chanel, Versace
or that catsuit on.

Maybe I am trying to start
a feminist movement,
if that's what it takes.
To teach little girls
you can be great
by simply being great.

Maybe I am trying to start
a race riot,
if that's what we need
so that the colour of your skin

doesn't determine
whether or not you succeed.

Being Black is not a choice;
it's a gift.

Being a woman is a lot more
than the anatomy you are born with.

Being a Black Woman?
That's a lot of pressure.

Diamonds are birthed from pressure,
and diamonds, they're forever.

Scan the QR code to watch
a video of this poem

IF I EVER HAD A DAUGHTER

I want to apologise
for that curse between your eyes.
If you are anything like me,
you'll be a prisoner of your mind.

I don't want you to have
this burden of creativity.
I want you to use logic
and think it out rationally.
The imagination can be a dark,
lonely place, so use it wisely.

So can the mirror.
But I will remind you
of how beautiful you are
every single day.
I'll keep my own
insecurities hidden away,
so you grow up with confidence
running through your bloodstream.
And a modesty,
so when people say
you're beautiful,
you're like, *Who, me?*

Even though
some of your beauty
lies on your skin,
real beauty comes
from within, so be a good
person. Free from prejudice,
intolerance and phobias.

I'll raise you under
the watchful eyes of God,
but you can call Her
whatever name you want.

Hopefully during your lifetime
religion will stop being used
as an excuse for killing
and bad politics.

I want you
to adore your daddy.
I wouldn't even mind
if you loved them
more than me;
it would assure me
that I picked the right one.
Someone you can see,
touch, grow,
feel, live in their love.

I wouldn't mind
coming second best
to someone who could
teach you the beauties
of loving and being loved,
and you give it a chance
because they would have
already shown you
how worthy you are.

You can love
whoever you want,
whenever you want,
however you want.
I'll be here
when it goes right
and I'll be here
when it goes wrong.

I might say it,
when you're naughty,
but know you could never
disappoint me,

even if you want to
live your life in mediocrity,
as long as you can
look me in the eyes
and tell me you're happy.
That's all I'll ever want you to be.

I may disagree with your choices,
but I will teach you to use your words.
I will teach you the power of them,
the implications of them,
the burden they carry.

But also the beauty of silence.
That there's no shame in crying,
but get yourself
back up,
no matter what;
pain is temporary.

I want you to read books
like the words will
run off the page.

I want you to know
the lyrics to the greats,
so, when an Erykah Badu song
comes on, you start singing along
like you were born in my day.

Baby girl, you're a queen,
and sometimes you'll forget.
Sometimes, you'll let people
take you for less.
If they don't want you
at your worst, baby,
they don't deserve you
at your best.

I was raised by queens.
Women who held entire families
on their back like a rucksack.

Women who were
born fighting,
born crying,
stay surviving.

Soon you'll realise
this world wasn't made for you.
Every hurdle that you leap,
they have leapt too.

My beautiful little girl,
if we ever get to meet,
know I've laid the stars
at your feet.
Step gracefully.

You've got the world
in your palms,
so never hold on
to anything too hard.

Know you'll always
have a home,
right here,
in my heart.

Scan the QR code to watch
a video of this poem

BURN

CS Lewis said,

> *Don't let your happiness*
> *depend on something*
> *you may lose,*

something that might leave.

That's why I refuse
to let you place
your happiness
in me.

I am a small fire.
My warmth
makes you forget,
when left,
I can destroy
everything you
worked to get.

I cannot be contained.
I will burn down everything
in my way.
In full blaze,
I'm the reason
the night
does not need
the day.

I do not want you to love me.
I do not want your promises.
I do not want your words.
I just want to burn.

To be so bright
that I can be seen.
Mostly, I want my
happiness to lie within me.

It is too fragile
to be placed into hands
that drop stuff.
It is not yet strong enough.

While I find my happiness in me,
yours cannot live here too.
When the wind blows, I move.
Don't let these flames catch you.

I'm too unpredictable to love.
Too free to be controlled.
What you might find beautiful today
will tear down walls tomorrow.

Your happiness
will not survive
this blazing heat.
I do not love.
I leave.

The scars will be how you remember me.

HUNGOVER

I wake up,
always fully clothed,
vodka dancing merrily in my system,
drowning out last night's bad decisions.

But I feel good.
In fact, I feel great.
It's only quarter past eight,
and my head's in the right place.

I haven't had enough sleep.
Soon my body will feel weak,
but for now I'm fine.
Staring at last night's glass of wine
I didn't drink before the taxi came.

Unsaved number
pops up in my phone.
I can't remember their name.
In fact, what name did I say?

Hop out of bed with a smile,
last night's tequila paving the way.

I must not have been
that drunk last night –
let me check my bag.
Phone. Purse.
Keys. No receipts,
can't remember what I spent
or what I had.

I'm not an empty glass kind of girl;
then I start to see my own reflection.

Fuck it.
I looked fly,
but SnapChat doesn't seem to agree.
SnapChat is not a representation of me!

Well,
maybe on the weekend?
Maybe with a few drinks in my system.
Maybe when I've let go of my inhibitions.

I've never woken up in a stranger's bed,
but I've woken up with the strangest head,
regretting a few things I may have said.
But it's easy to be misunderstood
when Bacardi tastes so good.

They say a drunk body speaks a sober mind,
but never in my sober life
have I wanted to ring
anyone at half five.

Shit.
I sent a drunken text.
I'm a drunken mess.
I don't even want my ex!

And now the room's started to spin.
This hangover is kicking in.

They say never mix your drinks,
but I'm not one to make a decision.
Do I want vodka?
Do I want brandy?
All I want is some clear vision.

I lost myself in the bottom of the glass;
vodka finds the fun side of me.

When I turn up, I forget about gravity.
Wake up and people are mad at me.
Vodka won't numb what saddens me.

I always say I'm never doing it again,
but what I mean is until next weekend.

Scan the QR code to watch
a video of this poem

AFFORDING JUSTICE

I do not want
to have to write
a poem for you.

I do not want
to watch you
bleeding out in the
street, or in your car.

I do not want
to see them
pin you to
the ground.

I do not want
them to use
only the top half
of a family
photograph
so they can
make you out to be
the devil, as it
fits in better with
their story.

I do not want
to have to light
a fire under this city
so everyone knows
what it feels
like to burn.

I do not want
to hear
I can't breathe
be your very
last words.

I do not want
them to put a
hashtag in front
of your name.

I do not want
a riot to be
your legacy.

I do not want
us to birth any
more parentless
children whose
skin make them
the enemy.

I do not want
to have the need
to justify my existence
with a catchy phrase.

I do not want
to have to explain
Black Lives Matter
doesn't mean that
all lives don't
again.

I do not want
to hear another
mother cry for
her baby on TV.

I do not want
to hear another
white man tell
me how I should
feel about my history.

They are trying to break us.

We can watch
our children die
on YouTube or
on our timelines.

They recreated
our jungles out
of concrete, but
our deaths aren't
worth the airtime.

Some may call it
police brutality or
systematic racism.
I have a hard time
calling it anything
other than genocide.

We were brought here
in chains and they're
confused because we
still wear them.

We were whipped
and now we buy whips,
live in cribs because our
growth scares them.

This revolution
will be televised
so it can't be
whitewashed
or swept over.
You can *B.E.T.*
that we will no longer
be bought by
slave owners.

If George Zimmerman
can be found not guilty,
then sell his gun to the
highest bidder,
look how far we've come
means that they've only
stopped, publicly,
calling us
niggers.

It took Doreen Lawrence
twenty years to get justice
for her son.

Sarah Reed
was 'found dead'
in her prison cell;
look how far
we've come.

If Malcolm and Martin
were here today,
would their words
still survive?

We don't just have
trigger fingers;
we have
Twitter fingers
out here
penetrating lives,
perpetuating lies.
We have become assistants
in our own demise.

I am not trying to write this poem again.

I do not want
us to have to bury
any more of
our women
or men.

I will not be
seen as a victim.
I refuse to be a victim
of this system.

You cannot cage a person,
degrade them, and still
demand their respect
and patience.

This movement
was a product
of frustration
and age-old racism.

We are not looking
for special treatment.

We just want to be
a part of a system
that isn't corrupted.

In lands where our
ancestors built the wealth,
when will we be able
to afford justice?

Scan the QR code to watch
a video of this poem

LOST BOYS

You will look up to
men who don't look
up to see the sky.

Fathers. Boys,
who wanted to
be men before
their time.

They act like trees,
parts of them leaf,
dropping apples
before they are ripe.
Here's to hoping
you roll free.

Every time your
mother tells you
you're just like
your dad, she's
affirming her own
self-fulfilling prophecy.

Trying to raise you
in the image of something
she has never seen.
Chalk outlines
fill the spaces
where your role
models should have been.

I hope you learn
to colour within
the lines.

I hope you realise
that what a real man
is cannot be defined.

I hope he has taught you
money will never
replace time.

I hope you'll be fine.

We make men
out of lost boys
and still expect them
to show us the way.

We put the crowns
of kings on the heads
of princes, hoping they
grow into them one day.

We love them.
We don't teach them
how to love themselves.

To be a man doesn't mean
you can't ask for help.

You are not defined
by how much
you can bench press.
How many people
you undress,
or the bottles
you use in the club
to impress.

You are defined
by your brain,
by what you say.

Being a man is what you can give,
not just what you can take.

I know that doesn't seem true
as that's not what the men
around you do,
but how you give love
is the most accurate
representation of you.

When you grow up,
grow upwards;
don't let your feet
touch the ground

Scan the QR code to watch
a video of this poem

HOME

I'm from a town
that everyone claims
to hate but no one
ever leaves.

Where you can have big dreams
but not always the means to achieve.

Where they knock down libraries
to build (un)affordable homes.

Yet the only letters
these kids know
are Z's and O's.

Where we light trees
rather than grow them.

Where it's cheaper to
feed your family at McDonald's
rather than the greengrocers.

The council spend so much money
on these new road systems,
but only navigate their youths
from their schools to their prisons.

They can start
a multi-million-pound
scheme and call
it 'regeneration'.

When more than 8,000
children are living in
poverty, I call that
gentrification.

Constant reminders
of no hope;
you can own
an iPhone
but you'll never own
your own home.

You can hop on a bus
and see how the Queen
lives. No trust funds;
trust alone is in deficit.

If money doesn't come
quick, it never comes.

A generation of
absent dads
and lost sons,
Instagram girls
and shit mums.

What's the benefit
in benefits
if nobody's benefitting?

When scales live in the living room
rather than in the kitchen?

You want to move?
No, wait, now you're
moving weight.
Are these the benefits
of living in Broken Britain?

I don't see how we can
so easily fail our youth
with alternative facts
and non-truths.
No positive representation
in the evening news.

They call us shit,
we fulfil that prophecy.

Between getting pregnant
and getting a job, only one
will secure you a property.

You can flip food in McDonald's
or flip food in these streets.
Either way, this system is
not designed for everyone to eat.
That is not because we're weak,
but because we don't have the means.

Eton and my high school were
not afforded the same luxuries.
We were 1.9 miles away,
but they are on like 9.1 times
my pay grade.

If you invest in the youth,
you make what they make.
Connect or tax man,
capitalism works the same way.

To regenerate something
means to grow from
damage and loss,
but at what cost?
Are we prepared
to write this whole
generation off?

Scan the QR code to watch
a video of this poem

ACKNOWLEDGEMENTS

To Bridget and Clive from the Burning Eye team – thank you for believing in my work, even when the entire thing changed. Your support and encouragement have changed the spoken word scene. To Hannah Gordon, none of this, and I really mean none, would have happened without you. Your guidance, your ideas, your support, is unwavering and I'm so grateful for everything – thank you. To Mum, Dad, Shak and Kenisha, who aren't entirely sure what I do, you're ROD and none of you know what you are riding or dying for. Thank you for always having my back - till the wheels fall off. To my Grandparents, who did everything but birth me. Thank you for all your stories, this pamphlet has always been for you. To Maddy, you just make everything better – thank you for loving me. To Annabelle, Tanya and Emma who put up with me tirelessly – Thank you for being family. To Bianca and Renice, with whom I have the world's best group chat, thank you sisters for continuously helping me recognise my magic. I will go to all the end of the earth for you to remind you of yours. To Rob and The Empoword Family, Charlie and the Word Up! family, Harry and George and the Word of Mouth LDN family – thank you for trusting me to create with you. Next stop? World Domination.

Lightning Source UK Ltd.
Milton Keynes UK
UKHW012247190421
382260UK00001B/120